HIJACK REALITY: DEPTFORD X

HIJACK REALITY: DEPTFORD X
A 'HOW TO' GUIDE TO ORGANIZE A REALLY TOP NOTCH ART FESTIVAL

BOB & ROBERTA SMITH
INTRODUCTION BY MATTHEW COLLINGS

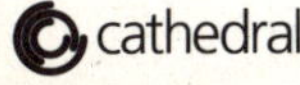

CT Editions

This book is published on the occasion
of the tenth anniversary of Deptford X,
26 September – 19 October 2008

With the generous support of
Cathedral Group

Board Members: *Chair* Dave Sullivan;
Treasurer John Jennings; *Directors* Ben Eastop,
Mark Davy, Bea Denton, Rebecca Maguire,
Liz May, Alma Tischler Wood
Project Director: Matthew Couper
Curator for 2008: Julia Alvarez
Project administrator: Shellie Holden
Advisor to Board: Andrew Carmichael
LBL Monitoring Officer: Kellie Blake

First published in the United Kingdom by
Deptford X Ltd, Creative Crypt, St John's
Church, 73 Waterloo Road, London SE1 8UD
Company number 04133414
Charity number 1087490

In association with CT Editions Ltd
47 Reid House, Hyndewood, London SE23 2BJ
cteditions.co.uk

ISBN 978-0-9547071-2-5

Distributed by Thames & Hudson Ltd,
181A High Holborn, London WC1V 7QX
thameshudson.co.uk

Produced for Deptford X by CT Bureau.
Edited by Christopher Dell. Designed by
Allon Kaye. Typography: Stratum by
Eric Olson/Process Type Foundry; Dolly by
Underware. Printed in Italy by Graphicom.

Page 2: APT Gallery, *Deptford X Showcase*, 2006. Courtesy APT Gallery

Artist who werent established Artist
Giving artists thing to do

OPEN SELECTION
— Where does came from

ART
BEARSPACE
WHALES
NOTICE
MOI
Lewisham Art House
(Depform)

ART
IS
GOOD
DEPTFORD X
HOW ORGANIZE A
REALLY GOOD
ART FESTIVAL

Developers
have
develope
the space

Studios

HOW TO ORGANIZE A HIGH QUALI
BUT INCLUDE EVERYONE

SELECTION.

KUNSTVEREIN

INCLUSION

EXCLUSION

FUNDING

How to get
involved

ART IN THE PUBLIC REALM

model of
how to do
things

emerging

Being
a Selector

PREFACE

Deptford X exists to promote the best contemporary visual art and celebrate that art with the widest possible audience – it is an arts event born of Deptford's creative community and based on a belief in the limitless potential of the area.

'Deptford X fell into my lap. It was May 1998 and I was finishing my Goddard's platter (pie, mash and liquor) when Rosalind Miller, a fellow "local" artist lent over. "Deptford's arty, let's have a festival – why don't you run it?" I ordered spotted dick and custard, then agreed.' Reuben Thurnhill, Director 1998–2003

All good art, regardless of its specific form, should have at its very centre, passion. Deptford X inspires passion, which is why it has become one of the longest running contemporary visual arts festivals in London. Artists care about Deptford X. They care about being included in the festival or excluded; and they will care about being mentioned, or not in this book.

The aim of Deptford X was, and still is, to show the best creative talent in Deptford, as well as to bring to the area the best of the rest. Luckily the best of Deptford happens to be very good. It was an ambitious project and to start it Reuben needed to build a team – so, like a lower division football manager, he scouted for local talent. Andrew Carmichael came in to help with fundraising, while the Museum of Installation provided some curatorial clout with Mike Ansell designing the initial look of Deptford X and Deb Astell fronting countless education projects and setting up an artist exchange programme in Berlin.

Over the years staff, artists and curators have run themselves ragged to deliver amazing projects with little or no money. Local arts organizsations, particularly the Museum of Installation, Lewisham Art House, APT, CBA, the Mornington Centre and ACME, were fantastically supportive.

Working notes for this book by Bob & Roberta Smith, 2008.
Courtesy Bob & Roberta Smith

Deptford X enthused people beyond the arts community – local council officers happily wrestled with all manner of unexpected proposals from having a stall on a market giving money away to sticking a car halfway up a tower block. By working on the edges of the gallery system (and often completely outside it) Deptford X was able to get art into the public domain. While Deptford X is on, art permeates everything.

Now in its tenth year we decided to celebrate our achievements, so Deptford X commissioned Bob & Roberta Smith and Matthew Collings to write this book. The former has first-hand knowledge of the event, while the latter comes to it with fresh eyes; both are highly regarded in their field. I accompanied Matthew Collings on a walk through Deptford and it was wonderful to see his preconceptions evaporate as we ambled through the streets.

We gave Smith and Collings a blank canvas, which is probably the best thing to do with artists, allowing them to express their thoughts (although not necessarily Deptford X's), freely.

You may think this book is controversial – and perhaps all good art should be – but I hope you enjoy and are inspired by the following pages.

Matthew Couper
Deptford X Project Director 2005–...

SPONSOR'S FOREWORD

We're really proud to be sponsoring this fantastic look back at ten years of creativity in Deptford. Deptford X has accomplished a lot since 1999 and we're very happy that we've been able to join in sometimes, help out sometimes and have a lot of fun many times. We were thrilled to be able to sponsor one of Spencer Tunick's famous photographic projects around the Cutty Sark in 2001. And this year we're really happy that part of the festival will be celebrated at The Deptford Project, the latest development in our growing friendship with Deptford Town Centre.

At Cathedral we need creative people around us to be able to do what we do, from the architects who design our buildings to the artists who help us make them even better; and from the people who make it all happen to the folks who live and work in the communities we build. We are nothing without their energy, vision, *joie de vivre* and creative madness. And that's why we love Deptford. Nowhere else could we have parked a 1960s train carriage, painted it in rainbow colours, filled it with great people and become such an instant part of a very happy community. We are inspired by Deptford, we're infected by the optimism and humour of the people we meet there every day, and we see a very long and happy future together. Here's to another ten years. At least.

Richard Upton
Chief Executive, Cathedral Group plc
cathedralgroup.com
thedeptfordproject.com

INTRODUCTION:
HOT SCENES ABROAD vs
THE GOOD OLD ORDINARY WORLD

MATTHEW COLLINGS

Leisure Pool
Library
peacocks

Bob & Roberta Smith is a great artist who was on the MA course at
Goldsmiths College in the year below me in the early 1990s. In some ways
the hierarchy has always been maintained: Bob enjoys the respect of
Tate Britain, but still whenever I bump into him I wish I had a thimbleful
of his charisma. In pride of place above my mantelpiece is one of his
works: 'TONY BLAIR IS A ZOMBIE OF DEATH', announces a sign in multi-
coloured letters in cheap gloss on a surface made of old boards found in
the street.

One day this work will turn up in a Christie's Dubai auction along
with abstracts by Egyptian artists overlaid with verses from the Qur'an
in Arabic calligraphy that go for record-breaking sums – second in
excitement only to paintings featuring pop-culture words like LOVE using
symbols from the Farsi language spelled out in Swarovski crystals on
black velvet. The market is going crazy over there. In the meantime here
I am introducing Bob's great words, which elegantly place the whole
Deptford X scenario in a context of urgent global concerns.

How better to pay homage to Bob and to Deptford than to return to the
events of one day in May, 2008, when Matthew, director of the festival,
took me on a tour of the town?

Surnames eluded me, I didn't know anybody and hadn't heard of
anything apart from random facts picked up on Google the night before.
But by the end of the day I had a rough festival mythology in my mind. Its
theme is twofold: A) Development: good or bad? B) Identity of Deptford X:
hot biennale like Venice, or exploration and celebration of real life of
Deptford and what's actually going on around us?

Deptford X's origins: ten years ago, some artists go to Lewisham
Council and say, 'Let's celebrate Deptford's arts'. The Council says, 'OK,
here's some money'. At that time there was a growing wariness about all
the development going on in the area. Lots of development is going on still
(is the perception) but nothing is quite in place yet. Consequently a slight

Katie Gilman, *Deadweight*, Deptford High Street, Deptford X, 2007.
Wooltop. Dimensions variable.

resentment towards the developers remains. They're too slow (I think of
Hales Gallery moving to Hoxton). And now Matthew is trying to build
up the vibe again, resisting a slight waning of confidence that might be
coming in by harnessing the smaller pockets of energy coming up –
the trick is to keep them going.

We're passing the Deptford Arms on the corner of the High Street.
It's just been taken over by some ex-Goldsmiths artists who've got an
exhibition space there. I'm enjoying looking at a sort of death mural on
a wall – Matthew says the Goldsmiths people project films onto another
wall nearby from the pub balcony.

We come up to an anchor that's been here for ages, a public monument
– an artist covered it in coloured wool for the 2007 festival, which had
the theme of INTERVENTION (this year's theme is CURRENCY). I ask
Matthew what the wool meant. He says he thinks it was 'transformation'.
'Hard and solid turns into soft and feminine', he says uncertainly.
The old anchor itself stands for Deptford's marine heritage.

An uncompleted grey mural of skyscrapers looms up. Its implications:
developers come in and now there's no space; in the past it was just
buildings being redeveloped, but now whole new buildings are going up;
all you ever experience is change, change, change. (The exception is the
High Street, which is the same now as it's been for fifty years, a bit of
working-class London – the development's all going on further out.)

We see the Seagar distillery, a great Victorian building. In the past
developers allowed Deptford X to have shows throughout the Seagar site,
but now a sign tells us it's being turned into STUNNING APARTMENTS.
There's going to be a tower just behind the Victorian façade (like Dubai
coming to Deptford). Continual change means that the festival has
constantly to find new sources of income and spaces. At the moment, the
developers are still on the same track as Deptford X, but soon development
will dry up: 'It's not a never-ending fabulous bonanza', says Matthew.

Bob & Roberta Smith, *Tony Blair is a Zombie of Death*, 2005.
Enamel on board. Photo: Lucy Biggs

I absorb ideas and beliefs. Shoreditch is the place of demons. Out there the developers are evil and not good. In Deptford everybody tries to find the balance between different interests, and so here you must think of developers as good not evil. I begin to see Deptford as a landscape of desire: everybody wants the landscape to fit his or her personal desires. You have to get on board with the right thoughts. The art people's thoughts can sometimes be negative. Their perception of the developers is that they want to see something good happening – surely they want Deptford to be a nice area not a grim one? And at that stage the developers are good for the arts. But once the STUNNING HOMES have been sold (the negative thought goes) you can fuck off. The way forward is to change the problem in your head and think positive.

Some of the developers – MacDonald Egan and Cathedral – have discovered long-term collaboration. Maybe they'll even provide a permanent Deptford X. The interest for them is the gentility, creativity and niceness of the area. But then there's resentment against this idea from

Charles Hayward with Joy Bonfield and Merlin Nova, *Herb Garden: recording for Resonance FM, weekend, second day*, 2004

people on lower incomes, including artists, who sometimes feel pressured
– they see another Canary Wharf situation, with pioneering artists pushed
out. (Canary Wharf was a great warehouse space in the 1970s and early 80s,
which having become artists' studios subsequently entirely lost its artistic
population.) As if to illustrate the point, we find ourselves passing a new,
still slightly unfinished, residential complex called OnesE8, which has a
gym and a swimming pool and its own security staff.

Again by pure accident we meet a musician, Charles Hayward, who
happens to be walking by. He's delighted to chat and agrees the war zone
mentality is the wrong one. He's an active campaigner for the arts in
Deptford. There's no real division, he says – mutual respect is all that's
needed. People confuse the trappings with the substance. The developers –
'They're just blokes!'

Matthew brings up Reuben whom he and Charles agree was the
original genius behind Deptford X. He brought in big names from the
hot art world. After a time another director came in, and she kept the
momentum going – in fact Hannah curated one of the best years, Matthew
says – 2005 – whose theme was EPHEMERAL CITIES. Simon Starling was
in it.

I'm drifting off at the vision of trendy art achievements (while saluting
the drive of the curators, of course). And I start philosophizing internally.
I think of art's inwardness, its connection to art history, and the difference
between that and its social role, its immediate use, and again the
difference between both of those and everyone's personal opportunism,
their careers. I think of the artists in the Middle East ordering up their
supplies of Swarovski crystals, and the ones round here signing up to
INTERVENTION, CURRENCY and EPHEMERAL CITIES. Dubai towers
going up behind the old listed Victorian façades. Matthew's saying there's
always got to be a balanced mix of big stars and local community –
you can't alienate the community.

Opposite: Creekside, 2008. Photo: Bernard Sims. Top: APT Gallery, *Deptford X Showcase*, 2006. Above: Mali Morris, *Degrees of Freedom*, 2005. Acrylic on canvas. 36×46 cm.

Deptford has a very high concentration of artists. But unlike
Shoreditch, there are few gallery spaces. There's no need to make Deptford
trendy: it already is that. The need instead is to address the perception that
it's far away. I certainly think of it as remote, as I've only ever got here via a
slow, frustrating drive from my home in Holloway. But it's only six minutes
on the train from London Bridge, and when the East London Line is
completed Deptford will be linked to my part of town by a ride of only
twenty minutes. Like Brooklyn to New York, maybe? Charles says he thinks
of it more like the Lower East Side, where he lived in the eighties when the
art scene there was really vibrant and full of originality.

Charles disappears and we walk past a seventies street mural. LOVE
OVER GOLD it says – Mark Knopfler once lived on the housing estate
opposite. Matthew says it was done with local residents working with a local
artist, and this sense of local ownership has meant that in its thirty-year
history there's never been any graffiti on the mural. It's next to Cockpit Arts,
a craft studio. (Although not part of the festival, which is devoted to fine
art not applied art, Cockpit plays an important role in the area's character.)

We're in Creekside, which runs down the side of Deptford Creek,
and over the past twenty years or so has developed into an area for artists
and designers. The Art in Perpetuity Trust took over a large warehouse
in 1995 and converted it into studios and the APT Gallery. Three great
contemporary painters work at APT: Geoff Rigden, Mali Morris and John
McLean. They're the reason I've been out to Deptford before, to see their
open studio shows during the festival. In different ways their work
connects to traditions in art that I can relate to and find moving.

Next to APT are three more studios: Cor Blimey Arts, Creekside Artists
and Arthub (formerly 'Framework'). A lot of floors in one building that
Matthew points to were empty when Deptford X started, so the festival took
over a whole block for exhibitions, but now they're nearly all taken up by
design companies.

Further along Creekside is an environmental centre. Among other functions it's a consciousness-raising place for school kids. They can go into the Creek in their wellies. This year Deptford X will put a work of art in the Creek, with the centre's support, and visitors will be able to walk past the bowels of boats and the tops of anchors. (The centre has offered space to the festival in the past, too.)

Most people in the Creekside studios live in Deptford but not all the Deptford X people are Deptford dwellers. There is, however, an award for this latter group sponsored by the development company, MacDonald Egan, and given during the festival.

Now we see an interesting sight: the Herzog & de Meuron-designed 'Laban', a conservatoire for contemporary dance, which won the Stirling Prize for Architecture in 2003. The building is set in artificially created low

rolling hills. The overall impression – the strange, pleasant, hazy-seeming surfaces of the building set off by a gentle green landscape – is delightful.

Laban used to occupy a space next to Goldsmiths, but it grew rapidly, so it came to Deptford and got this new space, with the site donated by Lewisham Council and the funding for the building raised locally. The whole area next to Laban, up to the Thames, has been redeveloped. In fact, over the last four or five years in the Creekside area there's been a very high level of development. Building sites and cranes surround Laban's placid green sweetness. In the Laban café Matthew introduces me to Andrew who runs a regeneration company (and helped set up APT in the mid-1990s).

As a regenerator, Andrew's initial aim was to unify all the different artists' studios. One problem has always been getting support and interest from Goldsmiths. A powerful signifier of the arts in the area, the college is too conflicted internally to get involved, and although there was once brief interest from the curating department, Deptford X couldn't provide the Rolls-Royce arrangements necessary for their projects. Andrew says festivals are curiously hard to sustain. Deptford X's main aim should be to generate art that responds to the area. Plus, it should have an all-year-round space so the festival is always the culmination of long-term artistic development. He and Matthew both agree that the overall theme of Deptford X is 'identity'. You have to work with what's already going on. You don't have to be another Venice Biennale – be Deptford X! Preserve its character as an area and keep being creative about how to get spaces for the festival. Talk strategically but act pragmatically.

'It all overlaps', he says: 'The more everyone talks to each other, the more you build a bond'. Remember, the Laban site used to be Lewisham's rubbish tip – from a lot of partners working together, you can get incredible changes. The artists' studios are here for good (APT owns the freehold), he says, so it's not like Shoreditch, where artists gentrify the area a bit and then are turfed out. Gentrification versus development

Top: The Deptford Project, Deptford High Street, 2008. Photo: Bernard Sims
Above: Deptford market. Courtesy Deptford X

Mia Fernandes, *Eat Me*, Deptford X, 2007. Installation at Manzes Pie and Mash shop.

versus creative people – it shouldn't be like that. Don't be in a war.
Get everything in harmony instead.

We leave him and walk past St Paul's Church with its impressive
Baroque spire. St Nicholas's Church nearby is where Marlowe is buried.
St Paul's will be a venue for Deptford X this year. Matthew has been doing
Deptford X for three years. At the time he joined there was a bit of hostility
towards the festival from local artists, who felt sidelined. Matthew was
brought in as a project manager, someone who could handle that side of
things: community engagement, generally looking after everybody and
making the egos balance. We're in the High Street. In Manzes Pie and
Mash shop there are some artworks on the wall from last year's festival.
A lot of the shops take part in it. My thoughts return to the Googling I did
last night:

*According to a unique mathematical formula devised for Yellow Pages,
Deptford in South East London has the capital's most diverse and vibrant high
street, beating more traditional shopping destinations such as Kensington High
Street, Oxford Street and Marylebone High Street with its ability to service
shoppers' needs.*

The exception to any sign of development in the High Street is the
Deptford Project. This is the old train station, now being turned into 'live
and work spaces', and a train carriage that opened as a café in June 2008.
The developers are Cathedral, who brought in Studio Myerscough (the
design group created by Morag Myerscough) to decorate the 1960's
commuter train carriage.

The High Street's market stalls take part in Deptford X. The festival has
worked with kids to get them to make artworks from bits and pieces found
in the stalls – the project was actually presented on one of them. Another
market project was *Fruit and Veg Chess*. I'm finding Matthew's warm-

heartedness inspiring. I tell myself, 'Don't be an individualist all your life!'
I see how a sense of community can be an extension of selfhood and not
the enemy of it. I think about that old anchor in the street. You've got to
reckon with people on all sides, and deal with their different egos. I admit I
shuddered at the idea of the coloured wool but now I'm thinking you've got
to take everything together, the twee with the tough, and make it all work.

We see a mural by 'Artmongers' showing a tie and a necklace and the
words HIS 'n' HERS – possibly the visually horriblest thing I've seen today.
And then we're at BEARSPACE gallery. I look at an installation inside: little
sewn figures in the form of kids with hoodies. The gallery boss, Julia, is
also this year's festival curator. She does all her arranging from her base at
BEARSPACE. She says a mix of emerging and established artists are shown
in the festival – this year Yinka Shonibare is in it as well as Matt Stokes.
I recalled my Googling session:

*Matt Stokes is an artist and film-maker. He had a residency at Grizedale
Arts in 2002 during which he researched the history of rave.*

This kind of thing usually makes me want to commit suicide. But I'm
totally into the community needs now. How about that CURRENCY theme
this year? Julia fills me in. It's demonstrated in different ways, she says.
The shadows and marks that currency leaves behind: Deptford's history of
shipbuilding, slavery and the first railway station; the market atmosphere.
These trades left their mark and now look at how all that industry is being
turned round into culture. See how artists respond to the area, and are
affected by it. What is their take on the future?

I'm loving the big-talking. The big theme now, Julia says, is History/
Future. For the last ten years, economically and culturally, there's been
a build up, and now Deptford seems to be at a turning point. Ten years
ago, in the YBA era, there were the empty warehouse spaces, the parties,

Harald Smykla, *Fruit and Veg Chess*, Deptford Market, Deptford X, 1999

Fruit Veg
Chess
Don't pay
play for it.

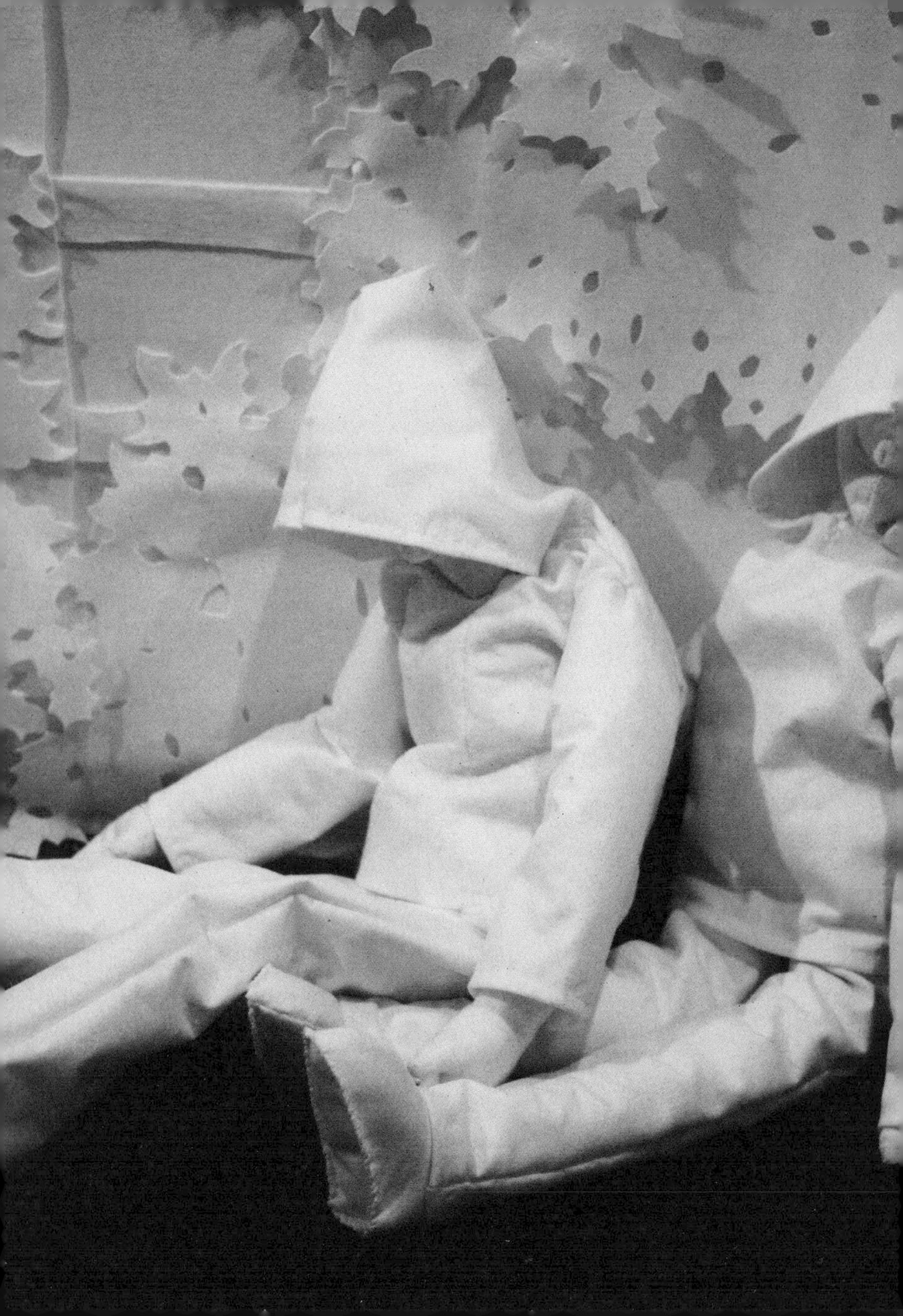

and so on. And now there's been development and money and interest in the whole structure of the scene. It's clear that Deptford could really take off, but it has to be done right. Deptford locals now buy art, in a small way still, admittedly, but there is real change in the social chemistry – the future will see a different attitude, more of a thriving creative industry scene.

Ideology and practical reality – Deptford as a place of trade – how do you get a creative industry to work, incorporating the concept of the market place, and everything that goes along with that? There's always going to be this tension with the developers, but they're now on the side of genuine regeneration and sympathetic development that preserves the humanity and authenticity of the area. Attitudes have changed, and developers now think it's useful to turn spaces over to artists and to art. Rather than chucking out the artists after they've gentrified the area, they're helping to gentrify it themselves – Laban, APT and others are here to stay.

And in all this change, Deptford X remains a big pull for the area, an integral part of its regeneration. So Deptford X has to build up these relationships. In fact, the festival is less like a biennale than an experimental art event, one where the unexpected is the norm, not a lot of predictable forms and rituals.

The tour concludes. I say goodbye to Matthew outside the Dog and Bell, the hangout of Jools Holland who used to live in Deptford. All the artists go there to network and also presumably to anaesthetize themselves after a day's striving to get a harmonious balance of power forces in the area. Before leaving me to make the incredibly tiring drive back home, Matthew says: 'Deptford X has taken time to be itself – it has only just started to feel comfortable.'

Paul Caton, *I Hear Thee Speak of a Better Land*, BEARSPACE, 2008.
White felt, pins. 200×200 cm, dolls approx. 70 cm.

A 'HOW TO' GUIDE TO ORGANIZE A REALLY TOP NOTCH ART FESTIVAL

BOB & ROBERTA SMITH

CATCHING THE ZEITGEIST OF DEPTFORD

My older sister Roberta had a friend who lived in Deptford. They had been at school together. 'Deptford Deborah' had a very deep voice and a kid. She played the guitar, smoked a lot and she was beautiful. I liked her. She had a strange charisma that older sisters' friends share. One day when I was nineteen Roberta said, 'Deborah wants to take you to see The Pretenders.' I asked, 'Why?' and my sister said, 'Well, now my kid brother has grown up, Deborah is interested.' Blimey, I thought, Chrissie Hynde and Deborah are quite similar. It's going to be a great night! But it never happened. I think all The Pretenders except Chrissie Hynde died or something, or Deborah thought better of it, or maybe she couldn't get a babysitter. Anyway, Deptford is still sexy in my book.

The lure of Deptford comes not only from this story of unrequited sexual initiation but also from the fact that Deptford is unusually arty. The famed Goldsmiths College lies at Deptford's heart. The Laban dance conservatoire opened their new building recently, and the hugely influential Hales Gallery once resided on Deptford High Street and put on important early shows with Jake and Dinos Chapman, Gavin Turk and Mike Nelson. But Deptford also has Deptford X. In truth, when compared with an Edinburgh Festival or the Venice Biennale, Deptford X is a modest art festival, but its programme has been well thought out, sustained and successful. Deptford X presents a model of how to organize a really top-notch art festival. The various organizers of the festival have had to wrestle with the big questions that face contemporary art: their solutions form the basis of the headings in this book.

Bea Denton, *Via Dolorosa* (detail), Deptford X, 2007.
Installation at Ha'Penny Hatch. Mixed media.

PSYCHO GEOGRAPHY: WHAT IS IT AND DOES IT REALLY MATTER?

Avoid the dodgy articles in *The Independent* by Will Self where he says things a bit like: '…I got a train to Thanet. I ran into my friend Antony Gormley. What a titan is Gormley! We decided to look for poor people together. East Kent is depressing. Glad to get home. Here is a scratchy drawing by Ralph Steadman.' His books are quite funny though. There is one with a shark in a tank on the front. Will Self was once an exhibit in the Deptford X festival. During the 2003 festival he was stationed at the Seager distillery writing a novel or maybe he put up a banner or something. Some people thought they could visit him and see him writing. Self is a mate of Mark McGowan, who is an interesting artist, so I suppose Self must be okay. Mark McGowan said he was going to drive up Ben Nevis with Self to make a Channel 4 documentary. I said, 'Tell me when it's on.'

A good place to research the world of 'Psycho Geography' are the films and books of Iain Sinclair. I can't remember if Deptford crops up in Sinclair's explorations of London but the idea that by exploring an area one uncovers not only the history of the place while reflecting upon your own situation is key to endeavours like Deptford X. Each year the organizers of Deptford X 'remap' the area. They invent a new cartography and locate artists' works and venues on it. These maps are invariably systematized in the modernist London Underground map mode. It is comforting to imagine art-world Baudelaires armed with these maps flanêuring around Deptford locating art works. I don't think I have ever done this effectively. On a Deptford X map from 1999 it says 'Deptford is the New Hoxton.' From the perspective of 2008, I don't think that dream came true. The point about the festival is that it is aspirational but also celebratory of the area 'warts and all'. The artists often like to work with the more desultory or eccentric manifestations of urban life. The maps present a psycho-geographic blueprint for a world that exists only in the mind of the curator. I think that's why they can be difficult to follow. I have been to Deptford hundreds of times and I feel I know the streets well but I can very quickly become disorientated if I try to follow the current Deptford X map – yet weirdly this is essential to the experience. The map with its key to events, artists' studios and venues is Dr Who's Tardis in which you have to fly in order to see the world anew.

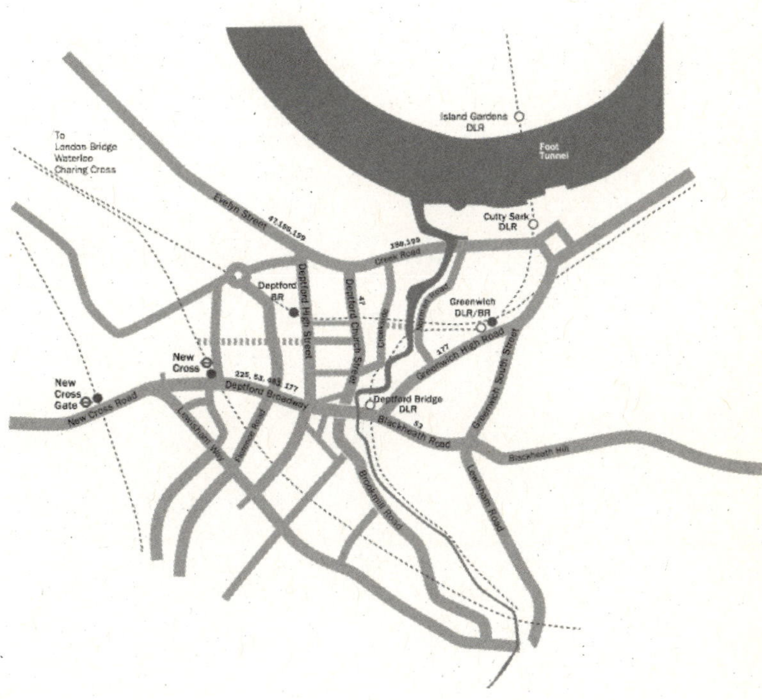

Map for Deptford X, 2007

WHAT IS A FESTIVAL?

Festivals can be a bore, enforced celebrations of things you're not interested in put together by people who don't much care about them either. They can also be playgrounds of desperation, writers all reading to one another, trying to find an audience when most of the audience wish they were in the spotlight. As I write this, there has just been a fly past of military jets. It must be the Queen's birthday or something. It becomes a festival of annoyance at a puny show of military might on a sunny London afternoon. In June and July there are now hundreds of festivals. Because the music industry has collapsed the only way musicians can make money is to play live. They are sponsored by drinks companies and everyone gets drunk. Weekend after weekend of people wallowing in mud, exchanging bodily fluids with strangers. The middle classes do it at Hay-on-*WHY?*. The young do it at Glasto. I don't go to any of them. The first thing in the recycling bin is the Saturday Guardian's 'Festival Supplement',

Charlbury British Legion Band, *c.* 1925. Courtesy Ron Prew and The Charlbury Museum.

quickly followed by the 'Jobs Supplement', the 'Money Supplement' and the 'Family Supplement'. Noël Coward said that television was for appearing on and not for watching. The same maxim can be applied to most festivals. Needless to say none of this applies to Deptford X. Deptford X is more like a fête than a festival.

A fête is a genuine expression of celebration of what is local alongside the yardstick of the 'more well known'. A fête does not seek the super overblown importance of the Biennale or the International Festival; rather it better serves the desires of its participants. In being more modest in its expectations, Deptford X allows a space for artists to experiment and try new approaches.

MAKE ART HAVE FUN

Deptford X is important because it promotes experimental and ephemeral approaches. Deptford X works with younger artists and gives them both a platform and a situation with which to respond. The curators of Deptford X do not know what will happen at the outset. Deptford X is a public Art Fête. Deptford X is a workshop. Deptford X is a hat to try on.

It is very important to really think about what the art festival is, and who it is for. This is 'A Tale of Two Biennales' – or, rather, a Biennale and a Triennial. In this year's odd battle between the Whitstable Biennale and the Folkestone Triennial, the Whitstable Biennale wins hands down. At a glance the two events might appear remarkably similar: both involve mainly temporary interventions in seaside towns by artists, and both have maps. You are invited to roam around the towns locating art. The Folkestone Triennial has more big-name artists, but the ethos of the Whitstable Biennale is better thought through and the work is more experimental than that of the bland presentation artists parachuted into

Overleaf: Lee Campbell, *Rise and Fall*, Whitstable Biennale, 2008. Main Beach, 17:15 performance. Photo: Simon Steven

Folkestone to ruminate on the town's history. The Whitstable event seeks
to introduce a new generation of artists both to a public and to each other.
Like Deptford X, the Whitstable Biennale invites artists to make a work
they have never made before. Both events give artists the space to work in
new ways. Never do the same thing twice, always experiment. In some
ways this argument mirrors *The Alternative vs The Mainstream Idea*. But I
know I would rather see someone I had never seen before work really hard
to make their voice heard in Whitstable or Deptford X than see some older
artist get his toenail clippings out in Folkestone. Though perhaps that's
a bit too hard on Folkestone – Mark Wallinger and Adam Chodzco made
interesting works.

GET THE KIDS INVOLVED

I have said this before and I will say it again: the people who work in the
education departments in galleries are much more interesting than the so-
called 'curators'. To put together education programmes means constantly
thinking about the art and what it will mean to people. Then you have to
go out and find young artists who have the time and hunger to work with
school kids. The education staff know the best young artists, and they know
how to think about what art is in a totally un-biennale way. The curators
just fly around from biennale to triennial thinking: 'I wonder if I can
persuade *that* Mexican or *this* Brazilian to come to Stoke or somewhere for
a show in December', while the 'education lot' have to deal with that shit.

The way I got interested in art was through one of these programmes.
I was a comprehensive school kid in a huge school in Wandsworth.
The art teacher sent me to the Whitechapel art gallery for a day school.
It was when Nicholas Serota was there and he had put together an amazing

Workshop with children from St Stephen's Primary School, Deptford, run by
Rebecca Carnihan for Lewisham Education Arts Network at APT Gallery as part
of the *Deptford X Showcase*, 2006.

Max Beckman show. Jenny Lomax, who is now the Director of Camden Arts Centre, was the education person. She told us about the paintings and Berlin then she said, 'Forget about what you have just seen and make a big drawing.' It was great. Jenny Lomax was always a fine-looking woman and still is. That day changed my life.

A humiliating thing happened to me recently. I was shortlisted to make a sculpture in Trafalgar Square, as part of the 'Fourth Plinth Project'. Because I have a dominant pedagogic gene, I got involved with the education programme attached to the project. I did a talk to teachers at the outset of the competition and recently the organizers invited me to attend the prize-giving for the 'Kids' Fourth Plinth Project'. The kids' prize-giving was timed to be a week before the announcement of the winner of the actual commission. I was a bit queasy about going because I knew that the organizers would already know who the winner was, but I thought it would look bad if I did not go, so I resolved to slope in the back of the auditorium and observe. However, when I got there Ekow Eshun, from the ICA, pulled me out and made me join him in giving out prizes to all the children, thirty-two in all. Ekow and I were photographed with each child. I thought, if I don't win this a lot of children will ask their mums and dads, 'Who is that strange man in the photograph?' To which mum would reply: 'Oh, some loser.' I asked one child what it was like to win the Fourth Plinth Prize. He just laughed.

Bob & Roberta Smith, Fourth Plinth proposal: *Make Art Not War*, 2008.
Photo by Leonardo Ulian

BERLIN THE BORING BIENNALE (ALL THE GREAT BUILDINGS HAVE BEEN BULLDOZED)

Deptford is suffering the same fate as Berlin. In 1995, I was invited by Waling Boers to show in his gallery in Berlin. Waling is a maverick curator and gallerist who had persuaded the Berlin authorities to give him the old Czechoslovakian Cultural Institute to have as a contemporary art gallery. He put on some pretty groundbreaking shows.

The Berlin Biennale was amazing that year. Not only was the art great but the buildings you visited were extraordinary. The opportunities for artists in Berlin back then were astounding. As an artist you could take over a former post office or old station and completely transform it. That moment has gone. In 2008 the Berlin Biennale had resorted to being located in two museums and a bit of waste ground. It was disappointing.

Because of its success, Deptford X faces the same problem. The un-let offices and railway arches that once provided interesting venues for artists have now all been let. This change in the fortunes of Deptford is to be welcomed although it means the organizers have to force the artists out into the real world. Mind you, this is something that Deptford X has always done. In 1999, when I took part, I was given a stall in the market on a Saturday. It was really good. On my stall I had lots of quite badly cast ducks and kittens. Close to mine there was a stall selling really beautifully painted versions of the same thing. The stallholder visited me and he said: 'Blimey mate, you'll never sell those.' However, later that day, an art collector turned up and bought 300 pounds' worth. The market trader could not believe it. I don't think he made that much all day.

Bob & Roberta Smith sell their £4.99 sculpture at Deptford X, 1999.
Photo courtesy Reuben Thurnhill

I PAYED
BOB & ROBERTA SMITH
£ 4.99
FOR THIS?

I PAYED
BOB & ROBERTA SMITH
£ 4.99
FOR THIS?

THE GATED COMMUNITY OF THE ART WORLD

The art world is a gated community. Many of the art world's initiatives represent a kind of 'Class War', but unlike the 'Class War' of the 1970s and 1980s, it is not a war against the rich but rather against the poor. Art has always been the expression of extreme wealth but there was a brief period from about 1947 until the YBA phenomenon in the mid-to-late 1990s, when social engagement and social mobility were taken seriously both by artists and by galleries.

Disappointment at the Labour Government's inability to close the gap between rich and poor is increased in the minds of people brought up to think of art as a liberating force by the recent actions and pronouncements of the YBAs and their gallerists.

Damien Hirst has implied that he will no longer exhibit his work for the public to enjoy. In the journey of the artwork from his studio to the Collector, the gallery has become redundant. Hirst's work now resembles the creations of a Fabergé egg maker. If art was ever the celebration of the artist's craft over materials, it is certainly no longer true in Hirst's case. Everything must be encrusted in diamonds and gold, all ideas must be super-banal.

Collectors and gallerists now demand that viewers make appointments and take their shoes off. The imagery of this new super-banal art is always the uncomplicated 'death'. Death has an instant look of importance but it is also apolitical. The Chapman Brothers do death. They do Hitler, but their work is based on a conceit that next time they will deal with a more contemporary evil – Osama perhaps – but they never do. They deal with Hitler as though John Cleese had never existed. Let's not get started on Antony Gormley and his traducing of the public realm to 'rusty industrial North' and 'climbing on plinths'.

The most successful artists of that bunch live in bunkers in the East End. They relax in private members' clubs with roof-top pools. They think up ideas on scraps of paper and have assistants take the scraps of paper to art model makers who then produce the work. They live a life quite unlike yours and mine.

But the cultural war is not just waged by the artists and their galleries: it also emanates from the education system. Oddly the creation of the huge Kafka-esque University of the Arts and the government's desire for 50 per cent of the population to go to university has had a divisive rather than uniting effect.

Art schools (if that term is not now redundant) are now big corporate organizations with huge budgets. Whoopee, you might think – but let's not open the champagne yet. The corporate institution has to operate in the corporate world. This means the language of merger and rationalization has superseded talk of education. A major art school is rumoured to be contemplating offering the students art education with no studio space – I recently met a tutor who said he was excited about the 'post-studio environment'! Overseas students who pay substantially more for their courses are flagged past worthy home students in admissions departments. Needless to say, the new Deans and Chancellors of these bodies are not artists or even academics, but businessmen who couldn't draw a plant pot.

Art has always been on the wrong side of the social divide. Art has never been for the people. Art exists now as it did for the Medici in the 15th century. Art is about social control and expression of wealth. Unless artists and the funders of art wake up and act, the period of social engagement in the arts, which spawned the likes of Joseph Beuys, Gustav Metzger and so on, will be over. As the post-war era ends, so does the belief that art can change the world. Worthwhile art will soon be dead.

I have painted a dark picture of YBA culture wrecking art. At the outset Damien Hirst and the rest were transcendent figures who gave power back to artists – but look what a useless appendix to celebrity culture they have all become. They are the court jesters at Tony Blair's investment bankers' ball.

This is not an argument for amateurism. Look at the Stuckists – who do they think they are? They are quite funny because they don't like the same artists I don't like but blimey their art isn't that good either. Their paintings look like Christmas cards the blind do to raise money at Easter. Sexton Ming is a good poet though and he is a better mover on stage than Billy Childish.

In the slow demise of art's desire to engage the public in any way other than to surprise us at its cost and to shock us at its subject matter, there are two significant exceptions. The first is Nicholas Serota. I think Tate Modern ought to be renamed 'The Serota'. Nicholas Serota is a visionary giant. In British art history there is no one to match him. John Ruskin, perhaps, and maybe Matthew Collings comes close, though Ruskin's talents of architecture and criticism were different. Serota is a political thinker whose thoughts are expressed through curatorial initiatives. Serota's vision to create Tate Modern is as important to British life as the post-war Attlee government's initiative to create the NHS. He is like a soft-spoken Vasari and what's more he is a nice guy who has a welcoming big handshake.

The second exception to the rule: I have slagged off Tony Blair's government for enlarging the university sector without proper consideration to what it would do to that delicate mechanism, the Art School. But they did get one thing right – 'tick-box culture' in relation to Arts Council funding of art and education. The current vogue is to attack the tick-box. Without getting too nitty gritty it is obvious to see why. If points are awarded to projects for ethnicity, disability, etc., you are already just a few steps away from only promoting artists who meet the criteria without regards to quality.

Joseph Beuys plants the first of his *7000 Oaks*, 1982. Photo: Dieter Schwerdtle. Courtesy Dieter Schwerdtle

The 'tick-box' approach also labels people and divides them, but what was good was that artists suddenly had to provide services. In the tick-box culture of the late 1990s education departments in galleries thrived. Education was now a revenue-creating rather than a revenue-losing sector within a public gallery. This factor encouraged artists to engage with the public. Artists suddenly had a role. Deptford X was born in that moment and its activities reflect a desire for art to be purposeful.

WHY DO ART IN THE FIRST PLACE? SOCIAL ENGAGEMENT

In the 1990s, the art world in Britain split, and the groovy YBAs were divorced from the Social Engagement Gang. The YBAs turned art into money and took centre stage in the media. Artists interested in a socially engaged art have also done quite well. The construction of Tate Modern and the Baltic, with their powerful education departments, the rise of the art festival (Deptford X really important and one of the first) and in France the publication of Nicolas Bourriaud's book *Relational Aesthetics* have all given artists who are interested in ideas and the public realm a useful space in which to operate.

Recently a friend of mine who works for a magazine called *Art Monthly* drew my attention to an article that used an image of mine to illustrate a point. There it was in glorious poorly scanned black and white, a painting of mine, *Make Your Own Damn Art*, photographed half-way up a wall. As I read the article I became perplexed. Dave Beech, who is a friend of mine, was attacking everything I hold dear. I wept. His main target was Bourriaud's book. His point was that it was too liberal, lazy and a poor manifesto for art students. Artists who engage the public patronize

Top: The Resonance FM booth at Frieze Art Fair, 2006. Works by Bob & Roberta Smith decorated the booth. Photo courtesy Bob & Roberta Smith. Above: Rirkrit Tiravanija, *Untitled (pad see-ew)*, 1992. Solo event held at SF MOMA, San Francisco, 2002. Woks, cooking utensils, ingredients for pad see-ew, glass display case. Dimensions variable. Courtesy Gavin Brown's enterprise, New York.

the public. I think he missed the point. Bourriaud was trying to identify something a generation of artists like Rirkrit Tiravanija were doing when they gave away Thai fish curry and got people to dance on disco floors. Bourriaud was not stating how art should be.

Dave Beech looks like a white-haired Elvis, but he was being a kind of Derek Hatton. Hatton attacked the Labour Party in the 1980s for not being radical enough while ignoring the fact that Thatcher was dividing the country. In our divided art world Dave Beech with his groovy sideburns, Bourriaud in his slip-on shoes and sexy accent, *Art Monthly*, Patricia Bickers, and even the 'super intellectual' Claire Bishop and Deptford X *are* on the same side. Dave Beech is on the interesting side against the boring, aging YBAs who have turned London's art world into 15th-century Florence – where art was locked away in chapels and gilded palaces and the populace go shit in the street.

Who are the interesting British artists? Well, there is Francis Bacon. He was Good. Susan Hiller, she is Good. Actually there are a few who are or have been Good: Phyllida Barlow, Helen Chadwick, Gustav Metzger (though he is technically stateless, he spends most of his time in the UK), Mark Wallinger, Ron Hasleden, Bill Culbert, Art and Language, Gary Stevens, Jessica Voorsanger, Bob & Roberta Smith, Tracey Emin, Jon Thompson, Gavin Turk, Jean Fisher, Ian Breakwell, Resonance FM and Ed Baxter, Carey Young, Derek Jarman, Juneau Projects, Lucia Nogueira, the film-maker John Smith, Jeremy Deller and Alan Kane (you may associate the last two with the YBAs but they are not) and Stephen Willats.

The above is not a exhaustive list of interesting British artists but it's a start. Now add your own name here .... Most of the above have made a commitment to art education at some point in their careers. The older ones and some of the dead ones spent years teaching the YBAs. Their work is characterized by its intellectual depth and its integrity; characteristics that simply don't exist in the world of the aging YBA.

ARTISTS ARE SOCIAL WORKERS, ART IS SOCIAL WORK

In the introduction to his book *Art and Social Function*, which my wife found in a charity shop for 30p yesterday, Stephen Willats states 'Art is dependent on society', and is, 'not the sole product of any one person.' 'The Audience is as important as the Artist', he claims; 'The Art work is a dynamic structure of events in time, dependant on exchanges between people reflecting their inherent relativity in perception.' Stephen Willats is an artist not a theorist. His work is refreshing because it is based in practice. He asks a question and finds an answer (of sorts) in the information he collects. His project, and many of the projects of the artists in the 1970s, was to radically occupy a new position for art outside the gallery and in society.

The YBAs, on the other hand, want to lazily inhabit a space outside society in the gallery – or just in their collectors' front rooms. That's why they are a bit crap. The project of Deptford X is rooted in ideas that emerged in the late 1960s and early 1970s.

Ian Breakwell, who was a kind of social engagement genius mixed up with Larkin-esque melancholy, worked on a groundbreaking project funded by the Arts Council called the Artist Placement Group. Breakwell was placed in a mental hospital (though this may not be the term generally used today). The experience was part of the job of the artist. It gave him access to a group of people he would never have encountered otherwise while giving him and his art a social purpose. The 'tick-boxism' of the 1990s and early 21st century led artists to say: 'We are not social workers', and, 'Art is not a cure for all social ills'. But in this they are wrong: they *are* social workers and art *can* cure social ills. All that art needs is real funding. Tate Modern shows the way. Let's build a 'National Art System', using Deptford X as an example. Here is how to do it:

Overleaf: Laura Braun and Jane Maxwell, *While You Wait*, Deptford X, 2007. Polaroids, 8.5×10.8 cm.

Your name: *John Francis Scher...*
Your object: ~~FREE~~ *FRUIT*
How and when do you hope to use it?

eat it

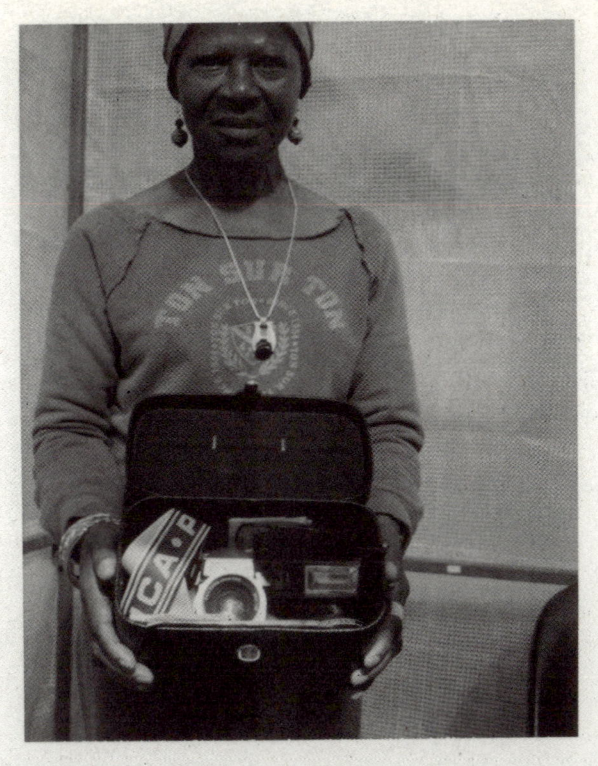

Your na me: TINA BLYTH
Your object: CAMERA
How a nd when do you hope to use it?

THIS CAMERA WAS A PRESENT
FROM A DEAR FRIEND, WHO
THOUGHT I HAD ASPIRATION,
OF BEING A PHOTOGRAPHER. 2005
NO SUCH LUCK. HA! HA!

DER KUNSTVEREIN

Since 1994, I have shown extensively in every part of Germany, in substantial buildings in city centres called 'Kunstverein'. The Kunstverein is an extraordinary organization that does not exist in this country. It is formed by guilds of artists, who first gathered together at the end of the 19th century to create a gallery space in which to show their work.

The Kunstverein in Karlsruhe is a grand Arts and Crafts building on three levels. Others are more modest. Artists in the town can become a member of the Kunstverein for an annual subscription. This entitles them to exhibit in a group show once a year. These shows can be like our Royal Academy's Summer Exhibition – some interesting work but overall a bit of a free for all. The rest of the time curators put on what they feel is interesting work.

What I like about the idea is that a service is provided for all artists whether they are old and a bit washed up like the YBAs, or young and groovy, or late bloomers. The institution provides a focus for artists, offering a structure for discussion. If we had a Kunstverein in every town with a groovy curator and an education team, think of the useful jobs for artists that would exist. Necessary work could be achieved. Let 10,000 Kunstvereins bloom. Let art be the evergreen language that renews our great nation!

Kunstverein, Atelier September, Karlsruhe, Germany

badischer kunstverein
Badischer Kunst-Verein

SELECTION (GETTING AN EXCITING LIST OF ARTISTS TOGETHER)

You have to let people do what they want. Goodwill is created by offering opportunities to artists and destroyed by weeding out the 'not so hot' ones. Every year there is a discussion at Deptford X about whether to hold an open competition of local artists. My advice is to include everyone. Two of my favourite exhibitions have been chaotic inclusions of everyone interested in making a work about a particular issue. *The Peace Show*, at Brick Lane Gallery in 2000, was based on the idea of the Greenham Common Peace Camp. Everyone who had a work was included. It was

The cover to the CD *The Apathy Band Live at Corsica Studios*, 2007. Artwork by Bob & Roberta Smith. Design by Leonardo Ulian. Courtesy Bob & Roberta Smith a groundbreaking event and a very busy opening. David Beech turned up in his pyjamas and recreated John and Yoko's bed-in.

The following year I was asked to design the graphics for the *Climate for Change* exhibition. *Climate for Change* was a massive show on four floors of an old factory in Southwark. The show was great and allowed everyone who wanted to make and show a work about climate change the opportunity to do so. It is ghastly and Orwellian when organizations that are set up to promote art become the gatekeepers of art. A few years ago, I formed The Apathy Band. We are a 'big jam band' – anyone can join in. Art should be like that, including everyone (even painters can be useful) for kiddies' workshops and so forth.

ART BAIT: THE LURE OF SOMEONE FAMOUS

Getting famous artists involved with your show just because they are well known is bad. They give you an 'art toenail clipping' and steal all the press (see earlier remarks about the Folkestone Triennial).

However, it is good to curate someone everyone has heard of if the work relates to the situation in a good way, or because that artist has a dynamic which it would be interesting for other artists to work with.

Themes can be good. *Margate Rocks: Art and Ecology* was good. Sometimes themes are rubbish. The curators who dreamt up *Pensi con la Menti* (or whatever it was) at the last Venice Biennale should be horsewhipped.

Overleaf: Dan Graham, *Two-Way Mirror Cylinder Inside Cube*, 1986–91.
The film, *Two-Way Mirror Cylinder Inside Cube*, 1992 was shown as part of
the Dan Graham film season at Deptford X in 2004. Courtesy the artist

OPPORTUNITIES FOR ARTISTS

Public money spent wisely can do several jobs at once. Money spent on art events delivers art to the people. It provides education, promotes self-awareness and gives a refuge to people on the outside of the mainstream. Money spent employing artists gives them a modest career structure. The young artist needs a role. Developing strategies to exhibit art is a challenge. Deptford X is an example of how dialogues are explored by generations of people in the same area.

HOW TO CREATE AN ARTIST BLACKLIST

I have an artist blacklist. I have not written this list down but it is there in the back of my brain. Curators are also on this list, as well as people who have blanked me at openings, anyone to do with the Fourth Plinth, Boris Johnson, Tony Blair and Lembit Opik.

When I think about it most people are on my list (though not my wife). Holding these lists is not a good idea. I say: 'delete your list and move on!' Not because people are not bastards, but because list-keeping drives you bonkers.

PAYMENTS

The best show I was ever in was called *Pimple Life*. The show was in Tokyo. We were paid a fee before we left England and I thought that was it. On the eleven-hour flight was Rebecca Warren, who was also in the show. When we arrived we were met by our Japanese assistants who would help us while we were there. They gave us each £3,000 in yen as spending money. Rebecca, Fergal Stapleton and an American artist called Chuck (or Chip, or something like that) had the best time ever. We stayed in the hotel where they filmed the mildly xenophobic and rather misogynistic *Lost in Translation*. The cocktails in the roof-top bar were expensive – a round would cost £250 – but it was good. When we got back home there was a further payment in our banks. That was the best show I have ever done. I can't remember what I did but I am sure it was good.

HIJACK REALITY

I was recently interviewed by Aaron Barschak. Aaron is better known as the 'Comedy Terrorist'. I don't know how he did it, but he smuggled himself into Prince William's birthday party dressed as Osama Bin Laden. He did his comedy routine and was arrested. Aaron also poured paint on the Chapman Brothers. Aaron was prosecuted. The judge asked him why he had thrown paint at them. Aaron replied: 'I would prefer it if you said "Why did you paint the Chapman Brothers?".' He went to gaol over that. Really, I should have been interviewing him.

Aaron said that I have three main areas of work: words, concrete and 'hijacking reality'. I said to him, 'hijacking reality is what you do'. Reality is being hijacked when you visit Deptford X. The idea that artists are

COMEDIUS
TERRORCHRISTUS
READY TO DIE
FOR
ALLAH
Calvin Classics

inserting themselves in the fabric of real life and claiming increasingly
large areas of it for themselves is a good one. Artists are 'hijacking reality'
rather than working with *Relational Aesthetics.*

Artists are all 'Andy Kaufman trying to make reality go a bit wrong'.
Andy Kaufman was an American comedian who appeared in the hugely
popular comedy *Taxi* in the late 1970s and early 1980s. Kaufman's career
outside of television was increasingly aberrant, and led him to wrestling
women, before his death (real or faked) in 1984. He is a popular point of
reference in the art world, though I think it's a bit delusional and self-
aggrandizing to quote Andy Kaufman: there were clearly mental health
issues behind those extremes of nihilistic comedy.

For many of the more interesting artists of the 1990s and 2000s,
the subversion of the public realm undertaken by Jeremy Deller, Marcus
Coates, Mark McGowan, Mel Brimfield and Sally O'Reilly is really exciting.
People are not being patronized by paternalistic 'relational art' – rather,
their minds are being warped and they are being 'hijacked' by art.
'Art hijacking' is good. Who wants to live in a world bound by stale
empirical truths? Actually, no one does. That's why religion is on the rise.
Oh God no.

We need to understand the awful truth. But let's make reality go
careering off the rails – not in a 1930s Germany sort of way, but in a
'futuristic landscape populated by windmills and houses with voltaic
panels', Archigram sort of way. Who were Archigram? Crazy 1960s
architects who believed buildings should be on legs (they're best known
for their Walking Cities). Look up Peter Cook. In this new world Deptford X
is a psychedelic art kidnapper. Like the Docklands Light Railway,
Deptford X is a drug that takes you places… man.

Aaron Barschak as Jesus dragging a cross along the Via Dolorosa in Jerusalem,
on Good Friday 2004. The performance was in protest against aspects of
Mel Gibson's film *The Passion of the Christ*. The reverse of the placard reads:
'Making a fool of myself in public is my passion.' Photo: Carlos Cicchelli

TRACEY IS GOOD

Thank god for Tracey Emin. Without Tracey anyone with even a hint of the 'Estuary' in their voice might as well give up. A few years ago I went to the ICA bookshop where they had cocktail stick flags on display. They had Tracey Emin's signature on them. Two Asian teenage girls were looking at them in awe and amazement. They bought two of them for quite a lot of money. I was impressed. The idea of Tracey was what had excited them. She was an icon for them. I know from teaching art to students in the East End of London that Tracey is a powerful role model. Her art is good too. The art world needs more Tracey and more people like that woman who paints pictures of Diana with a magenta face. They are good.

There are far too many upper-class idiots involved, artists who speak like Prince Charles. You have to remember if you are posh but stupid you used to have to be a priest. These days art schools are the refuge of the moneyed dyslexic. My sister went to a posh school. She was an only child for eight years and my mum and dad worked hard to send her to the Lycée Français. She loved it there. It is an amazing school. The teachers used to tell the kids: 'You are the top one per cent of the population'. She did very well.

By the time I came along, two kids later, my mum and dad were broke and I went to an enormous comprehensive in Wandsworth where there were stabbings. The teachers used to say if you work really hard, if you are lucky, you might get a job. It didn't bother me. I have never wanted a proper job. I think the problem with the big public schools is not that they offer opportunities to the well-off but that they give them unbelievable self-confidence out of all proportion to their ability. This is why we have Boris Johnson as Mayor. He believes he is capable of running London but it is clear, as he sacks one advisor after another, that really he hasn't got a clue.

Tracey Emin at the Art Car Boot Fair, in Vauxhall, London, 2008. Photo: Nick Cunnard

OOM
ES
LAB
COATS
LOVE
LOVE
LOVE
LOVE
LOVE
LOVE
LOVE
LOVE
LOVE
LOVE
LOVE

Why would he? He has no idea about the aspirations of Londoners because in the normal run of his life, up until now, he has never worked with them. Boris should have gone to art school. He could be making casts of his body by now. His Eton chums could be selling them to other Eton chums for loads of money. Other chums in the media could be 'bigging up' his work in magazines and calling the whole process 'culture'. The point of this is to say:

LET'S LAUNCH A MAOIST WAR ON THE CLEVER

is *not* a good idea. Art provides a meeting place where the British obsession with class is diluted. Art schools and events like Deptford X are 'social mobility interchanges'. The ability of art to be an interface between people from different backgrounds is recognized by Reuben Thurnhill (past Director of Deptford X, more on him later), Nicholas Serota, Iwona Blazwik and others in the public sector.

THE GOOD GALLERIST

The only interesting commercial galleries in the 1990s were Anthony Wilkinson Gallery (until I left them), Maureen Paley, Laure Genillard and Hales Gallery (after I joined them). These galleries seemed to look more towards Europe than New York for commercial models. In New York the position of the 'artist' in the scheme of things is marginal. Everything is organized around the 'collector' first, the 'gallery' second and the 'artist' third. This arrangement is born out of simple, pragmatic capitalist economics. It is hard to run an art gallery anywhere and in New York rents

Top: Beaconsfield, Exterior image from *Self Cancellation*, 2008. Beaconsfield © 2008.
Above: Pierogi Gallery, *Dewanatron Performance*, New Year's Eve, 2008.

are particularly high. The abundance of money for art in New York has led to a steady erosion of the power of the artist and to a rather boring relationship where the richest collectors are also the most important.

London in the 1990s was never like this. Artist-run spaces like City Racing, Bank and Beaconsfield provided an intellectual challenge to the commercial sector, which meant commercial galleries had to put on interesting shows to attract artists. The few collectors, including Charles Saatchi, were driven to collect works by younger artists.

The only American equivalent of the four interesting galleries in London listed above was the Ron Feldman Gallery, which consistently built a business out of showing difficult but outstanding artists. Feldman has been followed by the Pierogi Gallery in Brooklyn. Still, in New York it is rare to find galleries that have a serious programme based on anything other than financial imperative. The most telling sign that everything has gone wrong is when openings are populated not by artists but by smartly dressed wealthy kids who know less about art than most dogs do. Beware, London, and retreat to Deptford, where the market for art is unbelievably democratic.

REUBEN THURNHILL

Reuben Thurnhill is a good bloke. He ran Depford X for a considerable amount of time. He saved me a couple of times. Artists sometimes suggest some pretty stupid projects. Thurnhill's role was to encourage the edginess without actually causing legal problems. He asked me to design a T-shirt for the festival in 2001. In February that year the Taliban had destroyed some beautiful Buddhist statues in Bamiyan, Afghanistan. I thought it was crass and stupid to destroy art on this scale. I also thought how Rauschenberg famously erased one of De Kooning's drawings. Yet it struck me that in destroying

these beautiful and important religious icons, they were also unwittingly creating a conceptual art work. I came up with a slogan for the T-shirt: 'Viva Taliban! Pollock you are next'. Reuben said he would take the idea to the Deptford X board, but that it was probably unwise to go ahead. I was happy to come up with another idea. On the morning of 11 September, I was thankful that the inhabitants of Deptford were not wearing that T-shirt and that my name was not all over it.

Another time I organized an amnesty for bad art. Most of my projects have an element of 'I dare you to do this' about them. Reuben liked this idea a lot. *The Art Amnesty* playfully confronted head-on the festival's relationship with local artists. Most people understood that humour lay behind the idea. It was Reuben's idea to print a card with a personal declaration on it that could be filled in, pledging 'never to make art again'. After artists had signed the pledge they were given a badge stating: 'I am no longer an artist'. The local paper picked up on it and found an outraged artist who thought the project

was irresponsible. The whole project worked really well, with The Ken Ardley Playboys providing background music as we decommissined art materials and released artists back into the real world. Later I did the project in New York. I was attacked at the opening.

I work with Reuben at a university in London's East End. I asked him what the festival's legacy was for him, now he no longer runs it. He replied: 'Well I still get attacks of shingles from time to time.'

CREATE YOUR OWN REALITY

Although I have spent a good chunk of this book soiling my nest by insulting my YBA chums, I have to acknowledge the debt that the art world owes to Joshua Compston (1970–1996) and his invention *The Fête Worse than Death*. This was the first of the one-day art festivals that grew into the Whitstable Biennale, Beacon, *The Really Super Market* and *Make Your Own Damn Art World* at Mima in Middlesbrough, Gavin Turk and

Bob & Roberta Smith, *Art Amnesty*, Deptford X, 2002. 'I am No Longer an Artist' badges given out to participants who signed the pledge: 'I promise never to make art again.'

Deborah Curtis' Livestock Market and The House of Fairytales, The Art Car Boot Fair *and* Deptford X.

Joshua Compston put on three open-air events that changed how artists operated with their audience. In this book, I have tried to put forward the idea that the artists that taught the YBAs were more interesting than the YBAs themselves. And that artists need to re-engage with the real world in order to stop the art world becoming a rich ghetto.

Joshua Compston's importance was not recognized while he was alive. Perversely, the root of art's salvation lies in the legacy of one of the YBAs' major promoters. It took the YBA sensibility for brash popularism coupled with a Bukowski-esque underbelly to ignite this spark. Compston died not long after his last event, *The Hanging Picnic*. I met him in a café a week before he died. He was friendly and cheerful but we talked about how people didn't realize what he was trying to do and how difficult it was to fund his projects. It may be some consolation to those who knew him that somewhere between Compston's vision, Bourriaud's legacy and the radical positions of artists like Gustav Metzger, Susan Hiller and Stephen Willats, young artists are discovering how not to be dupes.

This afternoon I was at an event to raise awareness about Deborah Curtis and Gavin Turk's House of Fairytales. Dexter Dalwood told me a story about how a respected young dealer gave a talk at a large London college. Fifteen students stood up and shouted at him: 'We are not interested in what you have to say. You are the Enemy.' There is hope.

Opposite: Art Car Boot Fair, 2008. Photo: Nick Cunnard.
Above: Spencer Tunick, *London 1 (Deptford X)*, 2001.
C-Print mounted between plexiglass, 152.4×121.02 cm.
Courtesy the artist

EPILOGUE: GO TO THE PUB A LOT OR, AS THE ARTS COUNCIL CALL IT, PEER REVIEW

I went to Deptford. London Transport seems to be attempting to cut Deptford off from the rest of London, and the only route in was by bus or the DLR. Everyone on the DLR looked arty. Like me, they were all going to the Goldsmiths degree shows. Why is Goldsmiths so successful? The Fine Art department was once run by a visionary academic and artist called Jon Thompson. Instead of employing people who were no threat to his position, he employed (among others) conceptual artist Michael Craig-Martin. The two of them created an experimental department with no barriers between the different areas of painting, sculpture, photography, etc. Damien Hirst was one of their students. That was all twenty years ago. Thompson and Craig-Martin have moved on. The college has a brand spanking new building with an arty squiggle sculpture on the roof. It tells us that 'creatives' are at work.

All the major players of Deptford X were at the degree show, including Nicola Oxley and her partner Nico De Oliveira, who run Notice on Deptford High Street. In the entrance to Goldsmiths I ran into Ella Whitmarsh, director of Hales Gallery, who has helped organize large shows by Spencer Tunick and Andrew Bick.

The head of the Masters programme at Goldsmiths, Gerard Hemsworth, has his office in an old swimming baths. Gerard has two mantras that I remember from my time on the programme: 1. Go to the pub to discuss ideas after every tutorial; and 2. Stay visible!

The Apathy Band, including Roland Groenenboom (left), Leonardo Ulian (Centre), and Bob & Roberta Smith perform in front of Bob & Roberta Smith's installation *The Magninimous Cuckold Revisited*, ZKM Karlsruhr, 2007

hinter dem
baum
FRIDAY
THE HALL IT WAS A
MAN IN HIS
THEIR 30
MEN IN
TO SEE
BULLYING A BAND
BEING WATCHED BY
THEIR 40
IT
WAS A
PIS
BA
19 DECEMBER 1968
WHEN I WAS A CHILD I WAS AN
IN THE SCHOOL
PLAY NOT ONLY
WAS I LOST IN
THE FOREST I
FORGO
TURN
GRETE
BUT

I bumped into Julia Alvarez. Julia Alvarez is curating this year's Deptford X. She runs the impressive BEARSPACE gallery located on Deptford High Street. At the turn of the century her grandfather had a store on the High Street. Alvarez is busy organizing projects by Yinka Shonebare, Leo Fitzmaurice, Fran Cottell and Nicky Hirst, along with many other events and performances. She asked me to read *Hijack Reality* this year at Victor Mount's hapless celebration of hopelessness, *The Ding Dong Twist Club*.

Then I spied Reuben Thurnhill. Before us was one of the weirdest scenes since the last time I saw Reuben, when, along with 200 or so uptight artists and curators, we witnessed a performance by The Fall in the atrium of Bloomberg. Seeing Mark E Smith in that context was like seeing Picasso lecture a group of Sunday painters. It was a strange evening (Reuben didn't get home). Before us this evening, however, was a Korean student dressed as a building swooning to dreamy guitar music played by another student dressed as a New York skyscraper.

I asked Reuben which artist had he been most impressed by during his time as director of Deptford X. Reuben told me his favourite work was an elaborate installation depicting our solar system by Steven Pippin. Reuben told me he had also enjoyed putting on a gig of 'art bands' one year, including The Ken Ardley Playboys and Manchester band Die Kunst. Reuben now works with the drummer from Die Kunst, Richard Hylton, who himself is an *über*-curator. He said during Deptford X he would have artists shouting angrily outside his door at four o'clock in the morning.

I pictured Reuben as a kind of maverick, a South London Norman Rosenthal. Later on Reuben, Julia and I went to the pub. In the pub we met David Burrows and Simon Bedwell, formerly of the artists' group Bank. In this book sometimes I have written what *should* be true rather than what *is* true. I have depicted the YBA generation as an empire in decline, whereas hopefully many of them have their best work ahead of them.

I have characterized Deptford X as central to a counter movement of festivals and performances of a more democratic art impulse radically opposed to the gallery system. In my art world, Bank's show, *Zombie Golf* – where the artists showed their work alongside hastily constructed wax zombies on a floor covered in astroturf – was far more influential than *Sensation* at the Royal Academy. What is your art world like? Let's hope it's different from the *Evening Standard*'s art world.

FINALLY, FUNDING

Get some self-respect and don't waste your time (and the Arts Council's time) applying for money. If there is no money, get the artists to chip in. In the first show I organized after leaving Goldsmiths' MA, which was called *Something's Wrong* (and which was featured in *Blimey*, Matthew Collings' seminal book on the YBAs), each of us, including Matt, put in £50.

Bob & Roberta Smith are represented by Hales Gallery.

CONTRIBUTING ARTISTS
ACKNOWLEDGMENTS

Ekkehard Altenburger, *Camouflage Landscape*, 2002.
MDF and acrylic paint. 240×370 cm. Courtesy the artist

Peter Anderson, *Tom Waits*, *XPosure* Exhibition, London 2007. Courtesy the artist

FRED AYLWARD

FRANKO B

ALEX BAKER

SARAH BAKER

ANDY BALDWIN

BOLA BAMGBOYE

DANIEL BANACZEK

YASON BANAL

HELEN BARFF

SALLY BARKER

STEPHEN BARTLETT

SHUMON BASAR

JOHANNA BAUER

BASIL BEATTIE

SELMOH BBEW

LEANNE BELL

YOAV BEN-DAVID

PAUL BENJAMINS

MELINA BERKENWALD

BERNADETTE CORPORATION

LINDA BESEMER
GILLIAN BEST POWELL
SIMON BETTS
LOREN BEVAN
ANDREW BICK
ROLF BIER

David Aylward, *Part of One SE8 from the Ravensbourne – after J.D. Harding*, 2003.
Site-specific installation, digital print on PVC. 340×240 cm.

CHARLOTTE BINT

KJETLY BJORKE

BLAST THEORY

ROLAND BODEN

JOSHUA BOLCHOVER

STEPHEN BOLLARD

BONE

MICHAEL BONFIELD

ARNOLD BORGERTH *page 90*

ANNEKE BOSMA

ELEANOR BOWEN

NIGEL BOWLA

ANTHONY BOWNE

DAVID T BOWYER

MARTIN BOYCE

LAURE BRAUN

MICHAELA BRAUN

URS BRELTENSTEIN

RON BRIEFEL

TONY BROADWAY

Sarah Baker, *The Stud*, 2008. Video stills.

Arnold Borgerth, *Untitled* from the *Little Poems – Out of Nowhere* series, 2007.
Archival Chromium ink prints. 50×400 cm.

PETER BROMLEY

MATTHEW BROTHER-HOOD

ALAIN BUBLEX

RICK BUCKLEY

NATHANIEL BUDZINSKI

MICHAEL BURTON

JEREMY BUTLER

KEITH BUTLER

JONATHAN CALLAN pages 92–93, 94

LEE CAMBELL

NEIL CANNING

MATTHEW CAREY

BEVERLY CARTER

ANDREW CARMICHAEL

REBECCA CARNIHAN

CLAIRE CARTER

GIOVANNA MARIA CASETTA

SANTIAGO CASTANO

CATADRUFE

PAUL CATON

Overleaf: Jonathan Callan, *Empires*, 2003. Wood, fabric, silicone rubber.
500×250×10 cm. Courtesy the artist and BEARSPACE

ALEX CHALMERS

SUKI CHAN

CLARE CHAPMAN

JEFFREY CHARLES

CHARLEWORTH,
    LEWANDOWSKI & MANN

PAUL CHISHOLM

DUSA CHOI

DEEPA CHUDASAMA

LOUISE CLARKE

RACHEL CLAYDON

MARIA CLEMEN

STELLA CLIFFORD

BILL CLIFT

DIANE COATES

STEPHEN COCHRANE

PHIL COHEN

RICHARD COLE

COLLECTING LIVE ART

DEE COLLINGS

Opposite: Jonathan Callan, *Empires* (detail), 2003.
Wood, fabric, silicone rubber. Courtesy the artist and BEARSPACE

MATTHEW COLLINGS

COMMITTEE

CONTEMPORARY ART COLLECTIVE

MIKE CORNER

NICHOLAS CORNWELL

ALEXANDER COSTELLO

FRAN COTTELL

LOL COXHILL

MICHAEL CRAIG MARTIN

RICHARD CROW

PAUL CULLINANE

BEN CUMMINGS

DAEDALUS

KEVIN DAGG

CHARLES DANBY

DAVID DAVIES

PETER DAVIES

ROSALIND DAVIS

ALISON DAY

HARRIS DE KJAT

JENNIFER DEANS
DECKSPACE
HEATHER DEEDMAN

David Davies, *ROW 01, 21/09-27/10 2001. LED message display 200×10 cm.
Courtesy of Edward Woodman and Museum of Installation

SANTIAGO ESCOBAR

ALEX ETIMOV

JOHN EVANS

NICOLLE EVANS

TITUS FARNORTH

MARCIA FARQUHAR

JON FAWCETT

NEIL FERGUSON

ANANDA FERLAUTO

MIA FERNANDES

PATRICK FITZGERALD

LEO FITZMAURICE

KATE FLOOD

MARK FOLDS

FOREIGN INVESTMENT

RICHARD FORSTER

KIMBERLY FOSTER

CHRIS FRANCIS

Overleaf: Bea Denton, *Via Dolorosa* (detail), Deptford X, 2007.
Installation at Ha'Penny Hatch. Mixed media.

XIII

XII

JOHN FRANKLAND
GERALDINE FRANKLIN
TIM FRENCH
PIA FRIES
BEN FRIMET
ANN FRITH
ANTONY FROST
GORDON FURN
LEILA GALLOWAY
MILO GARCIA
CHARLIE GARNER
JAMIE GEORGE
CHARLOTTE GERARD
PIERRE GERARD
CHRIS GETLIFFE
JANE GIFFORD
KATIE GILMAN
GOKHAN
PETE GOMES
NEIL GOODWIN

Patricio Forrester, *Metaphor Sale*, Johnny's DIY shop, Deptford High Street, 2006.
Interventions on tools used metaphorically. Dimensions variable.

JOHNNY'S DIY &
BUILDING SUPPLIES
META
PHOR
SALE

SIMON GOODWIN
DAN GRAHAM
ALISON GRANT
JO GRAY
CAROLINE GREGORY
ANDREA GREGSON

Amanda Francis, *B.I.T (Bollard Icing Table)*, Johnny's DIY shop, Deptford High Street, 2000. Mixed media. Dimensions variable.

GREYWORLD

WIEBKE GRONEMEYER

ANTHONY GROSS

LUIS GUERREIRO

ADRIANO GUIMARAES

FERNANDO GUIMARAES

FLORENCIA GULLEN

ENVER GURSEV

ANITA GWYNN

CHARLES HADCOCK

JANA HALDRICH

GILL HALE

RACHEL HALE

MARILYN HALLAM

COLIN HALLIDAY

PAUL HALLIDAY

HENNA-RIKKA HALONEN

SHEENA HAMSON

ALEXIS HARDING

EDWARD HARPER

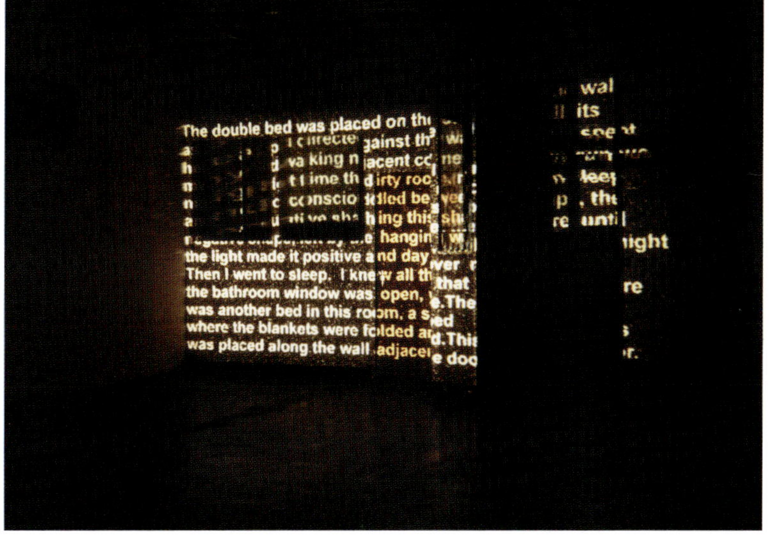

Liz Harrison, *Home*, 2001. Installation/sequential slide projection, 300×500 cm.
As shown in the *Fair Charm and Foul Play* exhibition, Deptford X, 2001

JOHN HODGES

FRANZ HOEFNER

KELDA HOLE

CHARLOTTE HOLLINSHEAD

SOPHIE HOPE

CLYDE HOPKINS

PAUL HOPKINS

JOHN HOYLAND

Margaret Higginson and pupils from Addey and Stanhope School, Deptford,
Travelling from the Past to the Future, 2007. Vinyl sign writers' materials, 16 window panels.

NEIL KELLY
DAVID KENDALL
BEN KIDGER
JAEMINI KIM
WARREN KING
MICHAEL KLEGA
ANITA KLEIN
THOMAS KLICKER
SUSANNE KOHLER
BORIS KREMER
ANDRAEA LACEY
NITIN LACHHANI
GRANT LAMBIE
LIANE LANG
RICHARD LANGFORD
SUE LAWES
CHRIS LAWLEY
ANN LAWLOR
NIAMH LAWLOR
RICHARD LAWRENCE

Max Hymes, *The Spiritualist*, 2007. Ceramic, various wood, beads, mirrors, pins, feathers, paint. 150×100×120 cm. Courtesy the artist

SAEM LEE
JANE LEIGHTON
LYN LEMONT-WEBB
LANIS LEVY
LEYENS
DOMINIC LEWIS
JON LEWIS
STEVE LEWIS
DAMIAN LIAMBIAS
ANNIE LIN
LITTLE ARTISTS
JANE LLOYD
REBECCA LOCKE
FIONA LORD
ANNA LORENZ
SUE LOWE
SEBASTIAN LOWSLEY-WILLIAMS
WAYNE LUCAS
KARIN LUDMANN
CHRIS LURCA

Wayne Lucas, *Self Portrait with Pepper*, 2007. Oil paint on canvas.
1219.20×914.400 cm. Courtesy the artist

CLAIRE CARTER MCCORMACK
PAUL MCDEVITT
DOM MCGLAUGHLIN
ROSEMARIE MCGOLDRICK
TONI MCGREACHAN

David Mach, *The Wild Bunch*, 1996. Courtesy the artist

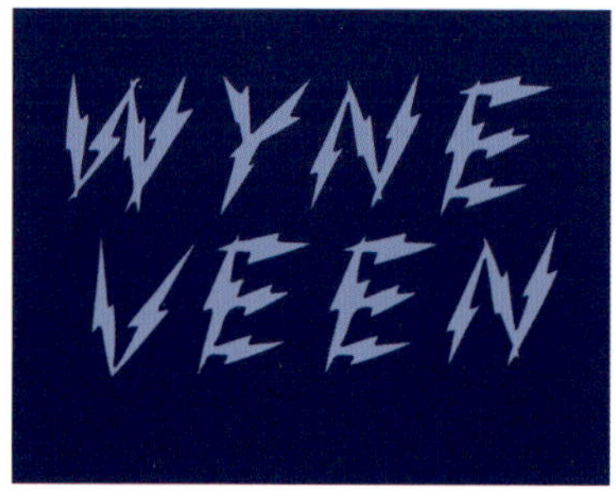

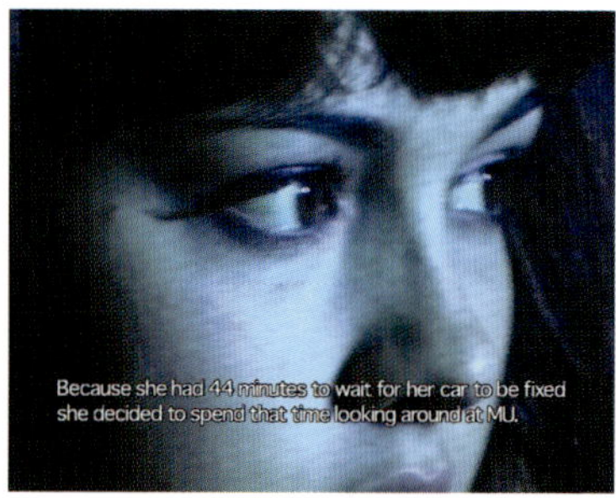

Miltos Manetas and Luuk Bouwman, *Wyne Veen*, 2004. Video stills. Courtesy Miltos Manetas

She finds contemporary art boring.

But one day, her car broke
outside of a place called MU in Eindhoven.

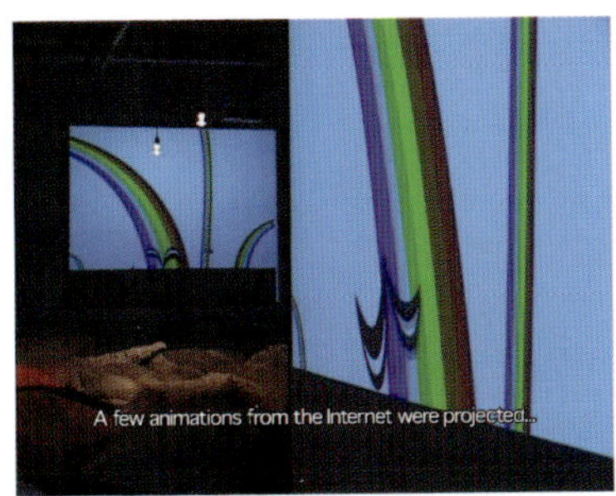
A few animations from the Internet were projected...

There was a guy who was making
the music we are now listening to.

Isabella Rozendaal was taking pictures.

GEORGINA MCINTYRE
ANITA MCKEOWN
REBECCA MCLYNN
PARTICK MEAGHER
LUCINDA METCALFE
ANA MIGUEL
STETLANA MIRCHEVA
STEPHEN MOLYNEUX
FERNANDA MONTEIRO
MALI MORRIS
ANNA MOSSMAN
GLENN MOTTERSHEAD
VICTOR MOUNT
AHMED MOUSTAFA
BRYAN MULVIHILL
KATE MURDOCH
DAVID MUSGRAVE
YOSHIKO NAGAI
CAROLINE NATZLER
JANINE NELSON

Chris Marshall, *Deptford Pink*, 2001. Two translucent banners sited
on Mumford Mill. 3×17 m. Photo courtesy the artist

NEUTRAL

DANIEL JAMES NEWNHAM

STAFAN NICOLAEV

OLAF NICOLAI

MAGGIE NICOLS

LAURANCE NOGA

IVON OATES

KARL OBULO

GARY O'DWYER

MONIKA OECHSLER

WILLEM OOREBEEK

JULIAN OPIE

KIRA O'REILLY

LUKE OXLEY

NICOLA OXLEY

EDUARDO PADILHA

HELEN PAILING

HELEN MORSE PALMER

KATE PALMER

MOLLY PALMER

STEPHEN PALMER
PANKOF BANK pages 122–123
KATE PARKER
NYE PARRY
SEAN PARTIFF
BRIGITTE PARUSEL
PETR PAVLIK
NAOMI PEARCE
MARK PEARSON
JULIA PECK
SIMON PENNEC
DANIEL PERLIN
MARTIN PFAHLER
CHARLIE PI
KATE PICKERING
FIONA PIENKOWSKA
CESARE PIETROIUSTI
PILOT
MARK PIMLOTT
SOFIE PINKETT

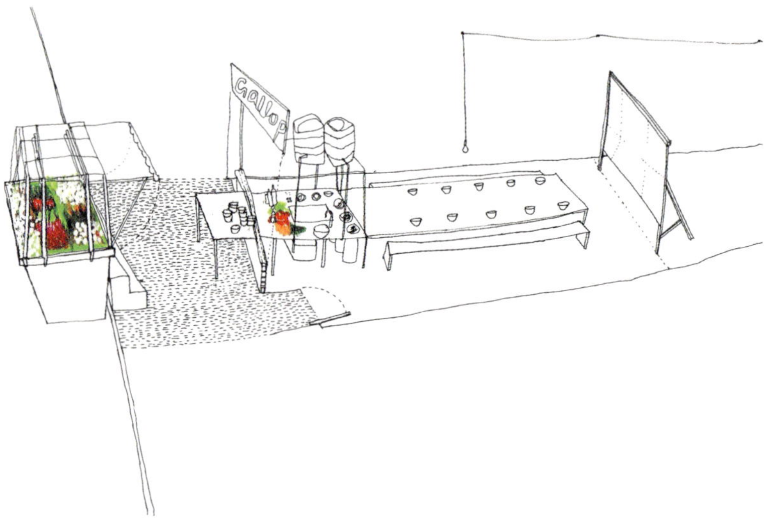

Pankof Bank, *Suppermarket*, Deptford High Street, 2006. Various recycled materials, organic material, skip, kitchen appliances.

American
PROFESSIONAL NA
American N
WEST L
TOULOUSE
SUP

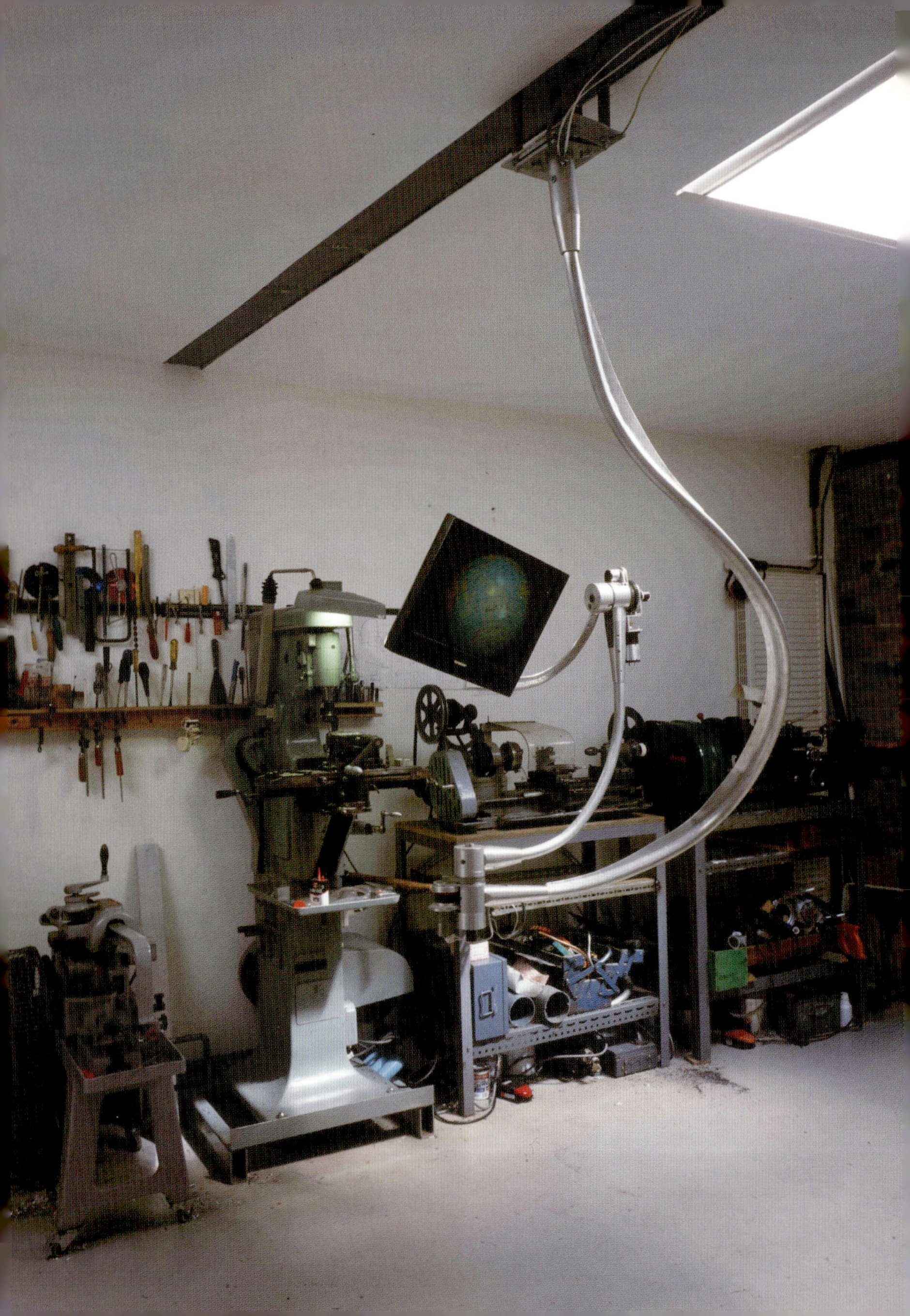

Steven Pippin, *Geostationary Flatscreen* (prototype) 2003. Flatscreen, aluminium, DVD player, electronic control system and motors. Courtesy the artist

DANNY RAVENCROFT

BEN RAVENSCROFT

COLIN RAY

CHRIS REINHARDT

SUZIE RENDELL

DAVID RHODES

KEV RICE

NICK RICHARDS

ANNETTE RICHARDSON

RAY RICHARDSON

EMMA RIDGWAY

ROBIN RIMBAUD (AKA SCANNER)

CAROLINE ROBERTS

JULIE ANNE ROBERTS

JO ROGERS

DANNY ROLPH

GWENDOLYN ROWLANDS

RAFAEL ROZENDAAL

ALI-SYED SACHA

HARRY SACHS

Harry Pye, *You just don't understand*, 2007. Acrylic on canvas. 50×40 cm. Courtesy the artist

GEORGIA SAGRI

SHERMAN SAM

JOANNA SANDS

ANDRE SANTANGELO

PETER SAUNDERS

RUBY SAVAGE

WILKEN SCHADE

CHRISTOPH SCHAFER

Robin Rimbaud (AKA scanner), *Track and Trace*, 2005

WENDY SMITH

HAROLD SMYKLA

JOSHUA SOFAER

LISA SOMINSKI

ARON SPALL

PETER STANNERS

SIMON STARLING page 132

Bob & Roberta Smith, *Artists Ruin it for Everyone*, 1997. Acrylic on Cotton. 200×200 cm.

MARY TAMBINI

SHELLY THEODORE

SAVINIEN-ZURI THOMAS

LAYTON THOMPSON

REUBEN THURNHILL

ALMA TISCHLER WOOD pages 138–139

ANTHEA TOORCHEN

SANDRA TRACEY

Simon Starling, *Cracked Tea Pot* (Wagenfeld), 2005. Lambda print. 82.5×67.5 cm, framed.
Edition of 10. Courtesy the artist and The Modern Institute/Toby Webster Ltd, Glasgow

NINA TRIVEDI
HIROMI TSUHU
KANA TSUJI
SARAH TURNER
SPENCER TUNICK
RUTH UGLOW
FLORIN UNGUREAU
DAVID UPSTILL
UTROPHIA
ARIADNE VAN DE VEN
JOSE ANTONIO VAZGUEZ
MANUEL VAZQUEZ
FRANCESCA VILALTA
MARTIN VINCENT
MAURICIO VINCENZI
CARL VON WEILER
DORA WADE
GAVIN WADE
SALLY WARD
NATALIE WASTNIDGE

SALLY WATERMAN
CHRIS WAYWELL
RACHEL WEBB
TOM WEBBER
KLAUS WEHNER
ROB WELCH
SUE WESTERGAARD
LAURA WHITE
MARRIANE WIE
JENNY WIGGINS
JANE WILBRAHAM
DAVID WILKINSON
SUE WILLIAMS
BEN MARK WILLIAMS
NICOLA WILLIS
KEITH WILSON
MELANIE WILSON
KITTY WINGATE
MARCUS WIRTHMANN
KERSTIN WITTENBRINK

Christine Stewart, *Maisie*, 1999. Marble with sandblasted text.
135×90×7 cm. Courtesy the artist.

BUTTERFLY CREAM CAKES

2 oz. margarine and lard.
2 oz. fine sugar.
1 egg, fresh or dried, reconstituted.
5 oz. flour.
Pinch of salt.
3/4 teaspoonful baking powder.
Milk to mix
Mock cream (see page 10).

Cream together the fat and sugar and gradually add the egg. Sieve in the dry ingredients and mix with a little milk to a soft dropping consistency. Three parts fill some greased bun or patty tins and bake in a moderately hot oven (400°F) for about 25 to 30 minutes until golden brown and firm to the touch. Cool on a rack. When almost cold cut a circle from the top of each cake with a small round cutter, remove and cut in half. Fill the centre of the cake with cream and decorate with the "wings."

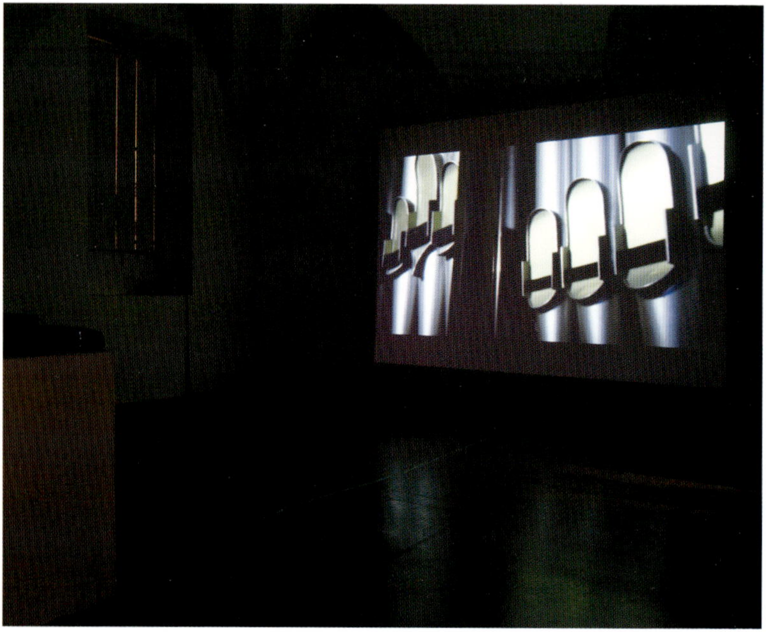

Matt Stokes, *Cipher*, 2006. Super 16mm film and audio transferred to Digibeta/DVD.
Commissioned by Collective Gallery, Edinburgh, Scotland. Courtesy the artist.

Following pages

Alma Tischler Wood, *Sky Blue*, 1999. Six 4.5 m discs painted on the ground. Norman Road, Greenwich. Kindly supported by bptw Partnership, Hilton Wharf, 30 Norman Road, London SE10. Courtesy the artist

John Wynne, *Fallender ton für 207 lautsprecher boxen (Falling tone for 207 speakers)*, 2Yk Galerie, Berlin, 2004. Sound, discarded loudspeakers, 8-channel amplifier, hard disc recorder, speaker wire. Courtesy the artist

Oliver Zwink, *Leck* (leak), 2000. Ink, watercolour, 400×200 cm. Courtesy the artist

ACKNOWLEDGMENTS

Deptford X would like to thank the following people and organizations who have contributed over the last ten years.

Board
Ellie Beedham
Clare Cooper
Richard Cryer
Bea Denton
Nico De Oliveira
Ben Eastop
Derek Hilyer
John Jennings
Rebecca Maguire
Nicky Malloy
Liz May
Wendy Neville
Dave Sullivan
Alma Tischler Wood

Steering Group
Kirsty Collander-Brown
Heather Deedman
Jim Delaney
Roanne Dods
Nick Edwards
Amanda Francis
Anna Harding
Paul Hedge
Margaret Higginson
Nico Ismay
Liz Leek
Gerry Marsh
Rachel Mellors
John Mitchell
Simon Rowe
Lou Smith
Miria Swain
Elizabeth Tarbet

Jeremy Wood
Leon Yates

Staff
Julia Alvarez
Mike Ansell
Deb Astell
Andrew Carmichael
Matthew Couper
Aldona Cunningham
Shellie Holden
Hannah Liley
Kirsten Lyle
Helen Maleed
Warren Morley
Gavin Ramsey
Kate Squires
Reuben Thurnhill
Sacha Walters

Sponsors

Public
Art of Regeneration
Arts Council England
Austrian Cultural Forum
Children's Fund
Community Education
  Lewisham
Community Fund
Creative Lewisham Agency
Creative Process
Creekside SRB
Deptford Challenge Trust
European Social Fund

Goldsmiths College
Greenwich Council
Greenwich Development
  Agency
Lane Castle
Lewisham Arts Service
Lewisham College
Lewisham Street Trading
London Borough of
  Lewisham
London Development
  Agency
Neighbourhood Renewal
Pepys Community Forum
Port of London Authority
Quadrant Housing Trust
Queen Elizabeth Hospital
  Arts Project
Regional Arts Lottery Fund
Skillswork
Slam
South Eastern Railways
South Greenwich
  Regeneration Agency
South London Business
South London and
  Maudsley Trust
Urban Renaissance

Private
AAPA
ACME
Advanced Graphics
APT
Arts Hub

Art Review
Atom
BEARSPACE
Balletgifts.com
Bowieart.com
bptw
britart.com
Brookmill Estates plc
Buddy's Cafe
Cathedral Group plc
CBA
Cockpit Arts
COG
Cogency
Concorde Digital
Cor Blimey Arts
Creekside Artists
Creekside Environmental
   Trust
Creekside Village
Deptford Arms
Deptford Arts Network
Deptford Train Station
Deckspace
Digital Fluid
Faircharm Trading Estate
Framework
Futurecity
Gallop
Goddards Pie and Mash
Goldsmiths Students'
   Union
Hales Gallery
Herb Garden
Hyde Housing Association
Inc Group
IPS
Johnny's DIY
Laban
LED Systems Ltd
Lewisham Art House
Lewisham Education Arts
   Network
Lewisham Shopping Centre

London & Quadrant
   Housing Trust
MacDonald Egan
MakeBelieve Arts
Mac Guffin and Shemp Ltd
Manzes Pie and Mash Shop
Mount Anvil
Museum of Installation
Mygate
Netscalibur
News International
Notice
Pankof Bank
Raw Nerve
Rhodes and Mann
Rubbish and Nasty
St John's Church, Waterloo
Scanlite Visual
   Communications Ltd
Screen Services
South Bank Centre
Spacia
Stephen Friedman Gallery
Stephen Laurence
   Charitable Trust
St James Homes
The Albany
The Birds Nest Public
   House
The Dog & Bell Public
   House
Utrophia
Workspace Group
Workplace Gallery

Supporters

Taiba Ahmad
Danielle Arnaud
Gavin Barlow
Kelly Blake
David Bowyer
Patrick Brown
David Brownlee

Steve Bullock
Tracie Couper
Liz Dart
Mark Davy
Lucy Diable
Steve Doel
Barney Drabble
Bill Ellson
Sarah Pfieffer
Eve Georgiou
Norman Goodman
Sue Gore
Nicholas Grimmer
Anita Gwynn
Jane Hendrie
Eve Lang
Carmel Langstaff
Lindon Lewis
Brigid Martin
Saima Mushtaq
Tony O'Leary
Sear Parfitt
Sarah Pffefier
Pete Pope
Gillian Best Powell
Hilary Renwick
Emma Ridgway
Joan Ruddock MP
Patrick Semple
Jake Stickland
Barry Sykes
Jennifer Taylor
Wayne Urquhart

The residents and
businesses of Deptford

And, of course, a huge
thank you to all the artists
who have taken part in
Deptford X over the years.